15-Minute Life Changers

GW00686334

Overcoming Redundancy

Peter Curran

Biography

Peter Curran is a Human Resources and Training Manager, having worked in the oil industry for 20 years. He has experienced several large redundancy rounds and worked both with individuals and management teams through these periods. He is married with two children and is a member of St John's, Stoke-next-Guildford.

Change – the Name of the Game?

We live in a world of change. This may come about through developments in society, inventions, progress, war or disaster. Or it may happen through the normal processes of living, working and growing older. The pace of change seems to be getting faster; its nature is less predictable and its effects are more dramatic. In the world of work new technology and increased global competition have meant for many people a loss of long-term job security, the pressure to become more flexible and the prospect (or reality) of redundancy.

How should we respond?

How should we react to change happening around us and often to us? We could resist it and attempt to carry on as before. However, this would be futile when change is inevitable and out of our control. We could attempt to ignore change, hoping that it will go away or pass us by, but this may only put off the day of reckoning and is rarely effective for long. An unquestioning acceptance of change is another reaction – what will be, will be. Some changes happen to us which we need to accept with grace, such as getting older. However, there are times when it is appropriate to challenge, or at least question the change occurring.

A more positive approach is to face change and become involved with it, hoping to harness it. Such an approach can make us partakers in, even makers of change, rather than people upon whom change is just thrust. We may conclude that resistance is plausible, or put thoughts of impending change to one side for a while, or accept it as appropriate. Through our involvement we are better able to influence change and manage its effects upon us. However, facing change is disturbing and difficult. Can we find some help?

Some things are unchanging

The Bible encourages change, but makes it clear that not all change we encounter will be comfortable (1 Peter 4:12). However, God will help us face it.

The Bible also emphasises things which are changeless: God's Word, His promises and character are described as unchanging and everlasting. Also, some of the fruits of God's work in our lives are of an enduring nature – love, hope and faith for example (1 Corinthians 13:13). The apostle Peter expresses the paradox well, quoting from Isaiah, he illustrates that while man's glory is temporary, Christians are born again into something lasting because of God's enduring Word (1 Peter 1:24–25).

For reflection and action

- Despite a world of dramatic change, your life rests secure in the arms of One who is changeless and can be relied upon.
- With God's help you can face change and influence it, knowing there is hope beyond it because God loves and cares for you.
- Read 1 Peter 1:17–25. What do these verses say about God and His world? For the changes affecting you, think of some ways of influencing them.

The Trauma of Redundancy

The Bible teaches that work is both good and necessary for our well-being. Just as Adam and Eve were put in the Garden "*to work it and take care of it*" (Genesis 2:15), such is our role in the world (see Genesis 1:28). We do this through our work and thereby take part in God's ongoing work. As such, work yields fulfilment and comradeship, provides for our material needs, enables us to serve others. Although it is made more difficult by human wrongdoing and the "fallenness" of our world (Genesis 3:17–19), it remains part of God's purpose for us. Therefore, it is not surprising that having our work taken away through redundancy causes us anguish and has the potential to harm us.

In a tunnel

Redundancy, unless truly voluntary, is a change thrust upon us. It often comes without much warning, and rarely with our involvement or consent and the effects are traumatic. As John Stott says, "It is a shocking experience to be declared 'redundant', and still worse to have to think of oneself thus." This is because it frustrates the good purposes of work; it threatens our material security, takes away fulfilment and brings our future expectations into question. For many, redundancy is like entering, through a gateway of shock, into a tunnel of uncertainty and downwardly spiralling self-esteem. The tunnel can easily lead through depression to despair, particularly if the resulting period of unemployment is prolonged.

How does our faith help?

How can faith in God help us through the change imposed on us by redundancy? What does the Bible have to say on such a change and our handling of it?

"He upholds the cause of the oppressed and gives food to the hungry." Psalm 146:7

Redundancy inevitably involves suffering. The Bible makes it clear that as Christians we are not immune from suffering. However, we can be sure that God will help us through it. Although difficult to see at the time, He uses it to good effect in our lives, as in a profound way, we share in the sufferings of Christ (1 Peter 4:12–13).

The Bible lays emphasis on the plight of the poor and oppressed. Those who experience redundancy can suffer oppression. This may not come from a tyrant or foreign power as in biblical examples, but from a society that creates and accepts unemployment. It may also come from organisations that treat employees poorly, putting increased profit before people. People can fall into poverty or remain in its snare through losing their jobs. The Bible commands generosity towards the poor and needy (Deuteronomy 15:11) and brings God's judgment on those who oppress the poor and deny them justice (Amos 2:6–7). God sides with those who are most vulnerable.

For reflection and action

- *Redundancy and unemployment frustrate the good and necessary purposes of work, causing the suffering and oppression you may be experiencing.*
- *God promises to help you through difficult times. Entrust yourself to Him, remembering that He is on your side when you feel oppressed and vulnerable.*
- *Read Isaiah 61; Luke 4:14–21. How do these verses reassure you of God's love when you feel oppressed and downtrodden? Entrust your situation to God.*

In Shock

Bad news which results in change for the worse can leave us in shock. We can feel numb, angry or deeply distressed. This can deepen as the truth of the situation sinks in.

Losing our job can be a most traumatic shock, whether it is unexpected or anticipated. Behind the shock is loss – initially of our job. This loss should not be underestimated, since its implications extend much wider. There are also many other things potentially lost – self-esteem, income, security, purpose, routine, comradeship and career.

The need to grieve

Redundancy has similarities with other life changes involving loss, such as bereavement, moving home, changing job. Following the loss of a loved one there is grief and a time of mourning before healing can start and the world can be faced again. This is part of the natural and necessary human process that enables us to come to terms with the loss and allows healing to occur. Parallels can be drawn between this and the loss brought through redundancy.

The Bible is clear on the need for expressing grief. King David grieved the loss of his friend Jonathan (2 Samuel 1:26). Many psalms express grief caused by difficulty, personal tragedy, persecution or defeat (e.g. Psalms 35, 38, 42). Jesus Himself showed His grief at the loss of His friend Lazarus (John 11:33–36). Jesus said: "*Blessed are those who mourn, for they will be comforted*" (Matthew 5:4). To express grief through mourning a loss is the appropriate and "blessed" thing to do, for through it comes comfort. God is the ultimate Comforter who, through His Spirit, comes to "*bind up the broken-hearted*" and "*comfort all who mourn*" (Isaiah 61:1, 2).

"Even though I walk through the valley of the shadow of death,
I will fear no evil, for you are with me; your rod and your staff,
they comfort me." Psalm 23:4

Grief is not to be confused with an ongoing state of depression or despair. Grieving is the necessary and important mechanism by which we express the deep sadness of our loss and thereby find comfort. It should not become a way of life. It is a cup to be lifted, drunk, then put down as we lay the loss to rest, so that we can then continue to live our lives again. We continue changed but not defeated, the healing process underway because of the time taken to express grief. Therefore we should not be surprised to be sad at our loss, nor be afraid of expressing it, in fact not to do so may mean that we have not really begun to come to terms with it. But in our sadness we must remind ourselves that all is not lost and that our God keeps His arms around us at these times.

For reflection and action

- *Do not resist feeling sad at the loss caused by redundancy, rather, express the grief felt inside, because therein lies the beginning of your comfort and healing.*

- *Life can be better faced when you have come to terms with the loss experienced. And remember, all is not lost.*

- *Read Psalm 23. Express the sadness of the loss you are experiencing to God. If possible, share the feelings of sadness with someone close who will listen and understand. Use Psalm 23 as reassurance of God's ongoing support and ask God to begin the healing within – aid this by listing some positive things which may result.*

Uncertainty

Change brings uncertainty. Redundancy would not be so hard to cope with if we knew how it would turn out. There is the uncertainty about what the company will do, then when redundancy is announced, there is the uncertainty of who will be affected. For those made redundant, the uncertainty then focuses on what may lie beyond. For those that remain, the uncertainty is not over as restructuring nearly always accompanies redundancies.

We all cope differently with uncertainty. Some can quickly adjust to new situations and prefer things to happen quickly. For others, time to adjust is necessary. Uncertainty disturbs us because planning for the future becomes difficult, life goes "on hold", we can feel we have lost control of our lives and we can become afraid because we do not know what will happen next.

These reactions are understandable. However, it is possible to find our way through them and, at the same time, find some certainties upon which to build.

Change of plan

We still have a future, however uncertain everything looks. It may be different to the one we expected, but it is still ours and still needs to be planned for. We may need to alter our plans, delay moving house or put off buying a new car. But we still need to plan in the short term (a job campaign, how we will use our time should unemployment come, and how the routine things of life will continue), as well as starting to prepare for the future.

> "For I know the plans I have for you," declares the Lord, "plans to prosper you and not to harm you, plans to give you hope and a future." Jeremiah 29:11

"God's master plan"

By starting to plan again we can overcome some of our feelings of helplessness. We can start to control our lives again, and do something positive. We can do this because we trust in God who is in overall control. He holds the "master plan" – we do our planning within this framework, seeking to align ourselves with His will for our lives. Proverbs 19:21 offers both reassurance and a warning: *"Many are the plans in a man's heart, but it is the Lord's purpose that prevails."* Jeremiah's letter to the Jewish exiles in Babylon seeks to reassure fearful people that despite their apparent helplessness and lack of a future, God has plans for them. He has plans for us also.

For reflection and action

- Despite the uncertainty caused by redundancy, God has a plan for you that gives you hope and a future; certainties on which to build.
- In the light of such reassurance, you can begin to plan again, reclaiming the initiative for your life under God as you seek what He has for you next.
- Read Hebrews 6:13–20. List the things you will need to do in preparation to begin the search for another job. Plan how you will spend the time not at work.

Overcoming Fear

"It's like looking into the abyss" was the frightened comment of one colleague not knowing whether her job would survive the current round of redundancies. An understandable reaction to the uncertainty caused by redundancy is fear. It may be fear of the unknown; "What will happen to me and my family? How will I find another job?"; or fear of what might happen: "Perhaps it will take a long time to find another job. We may have to move"; or fear of our worst nightmares occurring: "I will never work again. We will lose our home."

The shock and uncertainty caused by redundancy (or the threat of it) can make us very pessimistic and convinced our worst fears will be realised. This saps our energy and causes much anxiety. We feel the world is about to cave in on us.

Do not be afraid

Worst fears need challenging, as they can be hypothetical and may never actually happen. If our worst fear in relation to redundancy is losing our home, we need to calmly think through the likelihood of this happening. Having to sell my house because I have lost my job assumes I will have no money. Is that true? Probably not; I may have enough for three months or six months, or even longer. So what does the worst fear become? That the money will run out before I get another job. But how likely is that? Possible, but not certain, and there may be other sources of income. And so on. Such a process of challenge exposes some of our worst fears for what they are – problems that may not occur, or can be tackled over a period of time. It helps us get our fears into perspective and eliminates some of them altogether.

> **"When I am afraid, I will trust in you. In God, whose word I praise, in God I trust; I will not be afraid. What can mortal man do to me?" Psalm 56:3–4**

But given that real fears persist, how can we overcome them? We have a God who promises to be with us through our problems. He enables us to handle a difficult experience without fear because He is there. A child may be afraid to swim, but with a reassuring parent close by their fear can be overcome. God's message to the Jews in exile, dismayed and afraid for their future is similar: "*When you pass through the waters, I will be with you; and when you pass through the rivers, they will not sweep over you. ... Do not be afraid, for I am with you*" (Isaiah 43:2, 5).

Fear only leaves when there is trust to replace it. Our expression of confidence in and reliance upon God, is the trust that quashes fear. Our trust in God is based on the fact that He loves and cares for us, and wants the best for us (Romans 8:28). The way to overcome fear is to trust.

For reflection and action

- *Your fears need to be seen for what they are, and tackled in the knowledge that God, who has your best interests at heart, is with you.*
- *Trust in a God who is all-powerful, and who enables you to overcome fear.*
- *Read Psalm 46. Be encouraged by what this psalm teaches you about God's role when trouble is all around you, and about overcoming fear. Lay your fears before God in prayer.*

Paying the Bills

The world and its resources have been given by God for us to use responsibly in the provision of our needs (Genesis 1:28–30; 2:15–16). We meet these material needs by and large through our work. The apostle Paul advocates the principle of earning the bread we eat (2 Thessalonians 3:12). Not surprisingly, there is a strong association between having a job and our material security. If I lose my job, how will I pay the bills?

This fear cannot be lightly discounted. Receiving a wage means we can pay for food and shelter, clothes and the other necessities of life. Redundancy heralds a drop in regular income. This may be cushioned by a redundancy payment but this will not last forever. Belt tightening and real hardship may not be far away.

God is our security

God is the source of all things material. Even when the means are removed, God as the source remains. He can provide security at the most fundamental level, and ultimately, for eternity. He is able to muster any means to care for His creatures. This is the truth of many of the psalms. In Psalm 18, God is shown as a figure of security and refuge, a shield and deliverer from trouble and life-threatening danger. He is our ultimate and true source of security. Psalm 23 is a psalm of confidence and trust in God as the caring Shepherd. "I shall not be in want" (v.1) alludes to the experience of Israel in the desert for forty years where God provided for their needs.

"... do not worry"

Jesus taught how to avoid worrying about life's necessities: "*Therefore I tell you, do not worry about your life, what you will eat or drink; or about your body, what you will wear ... your heavenly Father knows that you need them. But seek first his kingdom and his righteousness, and all these things will be given to you as well"* (Matthew 6:25, 32–33).

Trusting God to provide does not mean we sit back and do nothing. While we are not to worry, that is not an excuse for inactivity. For God to be our fortress we need to act out our trust in Him; for Him to be our shepherd we need to follow Him; for Him to be our provider we need to actively seek His will for us. This is not a message of complacency, but a message of trust and of action. Part of this action is our search for the next job.

For reflection and action

- The basis of your true security is to be found in God.
- While the search for your next job goes on, trusting in God as provider helps overcome the anxiety associated with paying the bills.
- Read Matthew 6:25–34. Think what it means for you to seek God's kingdom first as you go about looking for your next job. In your prayers, hand over your worries and find the true security God offers to those who trust Him.

Restoring Self-Esteem

One of the most painful losses caused by redundancy is loss of self-esteem. To be made redundant is to be told that our skills are no longer required. It feels like being told we are no longer of value, as if we have been thrown on the scrap heap. In addition, our confidence can plummet when we no longer have a purposeful routine, when there is no need to dress smartly to go to work, when we feel guilty because we are not earning.

It is understandable that we feel some loss of self-esteem through losing our job. Work plays an important role in our development as people. As such it contributes to building our self-esteem and our confidence, as well as teaching us respect and esteem for the skills and abilities of others. What we do, particularly through our work, forms an important part of our character development and helps build our view of ourselves.

We are more than our work

However, if work is our only sense of worth and usefulness, redundancy results in a dramatic loss of self-esteem. Our society encourages such an association. We can all remember well-meaning aunts and uncles asking us when we were children what we wanted to be when we grew up. The implication being that our work defines who we are, not just what we do. The language we use to describe our work often reinforces this perception: "I'm a doctor"; "I'm a fitter". The obvious danger is that we allow all that we are to be defined by our work. Hence when our work is taken away, so is our self-esteem.

Valuable to God

Work is an important and necessary ingredient to our lives. It contributes to our self-esteem, but should not be the fundamental basis of it. Our true self-esteem comes from the value and worth invested in us by God, not from what we do or have achieved. Above all, we are created in God's image and precious to Him. God loves each one of us so much that He sent Jesus to save us through His death and resurrection (John 3:16). This love is available to us all whatever our situation, reaching us when and where we least expect it (Ephesians 2:4–5).

To Paul's statement of oneness in Christ: "*There is neither Jew nor Greek, slave nor free, male nor female ...*" (Galatians 3:28), we might add "employed nor unemployed". This is one of our society's major divisions, perhaps its biggest division of the future. Self-esteem through Christ comes from equal sonship before God (Galatians 3:26), not from worth measured by earthly job or status.

For reflection and action

- Although work contributes to your self-esteem, it is not the fundamental basis of it. Redundancy does not redefine who you are, but is a redirection of what you do.

- You are loved and valued by God, and this is the fundamental source and measure of your self-esteem. Your view of yourself should be based on this fact.

- Read Isaiah 43:1–7. Use these verses to reflect on the value God places on your life. As someone created for God's glory (v.7), ask for His direction on how to use your life in the future.

Taking the Strain

Facing redundancy is stressful because of the uncertainty and change it brings. The uncertainty can begin as soon as jobs are threatened and continues after a person is made redundant. The stress and uncertainty prior to redundancy can be so intense that some people feel relieved when their fate is actually confirmed.

Redundancy

Losing our job comes high up on the list of stresses caused by major life changes. It can also precipitate other major changes such as a lowering of income, moving house or starting a new job. These can occur close together, and all bring their own stress. It can feel as if the world is closing in on us and we can become consumed with worry.

A certain level of stress gives us challenge and brings out the best in us. If we were never faced with a deadline, or a test, or a difficulty to overcome, we would not develop our skills and personalities. Under such pressure, we respond both physically (adrenaline pumps) and psychologically (we "move up a gear") to cope. However, a consistently high level of stress can be dangerous as it demands such responses from us continually. It can then wear down our emotions through worry, and denude our health through sleepless nights, tiredness, the constant nervous "butterflies in the stomach" feeling, or worse.

Handling stress

We need to take care of ourselves and take practical steps to deal with stress. Exercise is a natural way of releasing "pent-up" tension; not necessarily sport, but just a walk can help. This can also provide a healthy distraction from our constant focus on problems. Diet is an area to check, as stress can cause us to over or under eat. We also need to ensure we get sufficient sleep. Regular exercise, a balanced diet and sufficient sleep will help us cope better.

Talking about the things which concern us helps us handle the worry that stress brings. Sharing our concerns instead of dwelling on them in itself can bring us a sense of relief.

It can also help us see our problems from a different perspective, and enables others to help.

Above all, we need to understand that our problems are important to God. What concerns us, is of concern to Him. God's message to King Jehoshaphat when faced by the armies of Moab and Ammon is relevant to us as we face seemingly insurmountable odds: "*Do not be afraid or discouraged because of this vast army. For the battle is not yours, but God's*" (2 Chronicles 20:15).

God does not promise to make our problems disappear. He wants to help us through them and take the anxiety from us. Yoked to Him, the burden of stress is shared, the worry dissipated, and we find some rest in the midst of troubled times (Matthew 11:28–30).

For reflection and action

- Stress can be reduced through exercise, good diet, sleep and sharing our troubles with others.
- God offers to help shoulder our burdens and take away our anxiety about them.
- Read 2 Corinthians 4:7–18. Paul speaks of being hard pressed on every side, but not crushed. Consider how, with God's help, you can handle the pressures you are facing.

Down But Not Out

After the initial shock of being made redundant, any hopefulness we may feel, with disappointments, can easily descend into depression. This can deepen if the time spent unemployed continues. Depression reduces our emotional well-being and we can feel continually sad, hopeless, pessimistic and lose interest in life. This often lowers our self-esteem and confidence, and makes it even harder to motivate ourselves in our job search.

Climbing back up

The end point of deepening depression is despair. If our search for another job continues without success, we can become thoroughly demoralised and engulfed by a sense of utter hopelessness. Once we fall into depression and despair, it is difficult to climb out; like deep mud they entrap us and suck us further down.

The Bible is refreshingly honest when things are not going well. Many passages express the depression and despair caused by great loss that appears to shut off the future. The despair of Jewish exiles in Babylon is summed up in Psalm 137: "*By the rivers of Babylon we sat and wept when we remembered Zion*" (v.1). When depressed and despairing the tendency is to want to turn the clock back to better times, to restore the past through remembrance, as if that is where hope lies. Or we may feel, like the writer of Psalm 22, that God has deserted us: "*My God, my God, why have you forsaken me?*" (v.1). The psalmist goes on to recognise God as His help and source of strength, after expressing openly and honestly how he actually feels when depressed and in despair.

The door of hope

The way back from depression and despair is through the door of hope – hope that again reassures us of our future. In Psalm 42, the psalmist expresses how downcast he feels, and finds the answer "*Put your hope in

God" (v.5). This hope is based on the psalmist's experience of God in the past, and helps him look to the future: "*for I will yet praise him*" (vv.5, 11). It does not avoid the difficult questions we ask, particularly when depressed, such as "*why doesn't God appear to be helping me?*" (vv.1–3, 9–10). Like the psalmist, we need to express how we feel, while holding on to the hope given to us by a trustworthy God. This hope is a confident expectation that God has a future for us and that He will help us grasp it despite current problems.

For reflection and action

- Redundancy may have led you into the trap of depression and despair. However, there is a way back, a door of hope.
- This hope is in God and is based on His trustworthiness. It can be rekindled by reflecting on past experiences of His help. Such hope can sustain you in the present and help direct you towards the future.
- Read Psalm 42. Use this psalm as a tool to express your own feelings before God when depressed and despairing. List some key difficulties He has helped you through in the past, and use these as a springboard to ask for His help now.

Past My Sell-By Date?

Being made redundant can make us feel useless, worthless or even like being on the scrap heap. Our skills are not required by the organisation any more, and what can make matters worse is that the skills used in our previous job may not now be needed by any organisation if the whole industry has relocated, been automated or is in decline. A colleague summed up his feelings when news of redundancy came: "I'm past my sell-by date." Our current skill may no longer be required, but we each have underlying skills that can be transferred to another job, or transformed or added to.

Review your skills

A compost heap may not seem much better than a scrap heap – both are places where things past their usefulness in their current form are placed. However, on the compost heap things get transformed then re-used back in the garden. Our skills may need transforming so that they become useful again back in the workplace.

Each of us has underlying skills that we could use in another job – our transferable skills. These may be an ability to communicate well, a skill with our hands, an aptitude for figures, an ability to motivate others, a skill at organising, etc. Their mix and competence are something unique to us, and even if our main professional or technical skill is no longer required, we will be able to use these transferable skills.

Some of our skills are in need of transformation. This means adapting them and applying them in new ways. For example, a garage mechanic may apply his knowledge of engines to teach motor mechanics in a college, an oil geologist may adapt his experience of drilling and rocks to work for a company drilling water wells.

We may also need to acquire new skills. This does not undermine our existing skills as they are a good foundation of experience to build on. But we need to equip ourselves with skills which are needed in the workplace. It is a reminder to us that life is a continual learning process and that we are never too old to learn – it is possible to teach old dogs new tricks!

Transformed and re-used

The picture of the compost heap, of things being reclaimed, transformed and used again, reminds us of God's work. He redeems and transforms our lives. He offers us forgiveness and eternal life, making us more Christ-like as we follow Him. God came as Redeemer to the exiled Jews who were thrown on the scrap heap as a defeated people, having lost their land, livelihood and self-esteem. He promised to restore them to their land so that they would again give Him glory (Isaiah 43:1–7). God is also our Redeemer, minding us through troubled times, and restoring us so that we can again use our skills to His glory.

For reflection and action

* You have skills that can be transferred, transformed and added to.
* God, the eternal Redeemer, is interested in redeeming you and your skills for useful work in His service.
* Read Isaiah 43:1–7. List the skills you have which could be transferred to another job, and those which need transforming. Decide how you will go about acquiring any new skills you may need.

Faith to Go Forward

The shock of redundancy, its uncertainty and the fears it brings, all have to be faced and managed in one way or another. So do the knocks to security and self-esteem, stress and anxiety, even depression and despair. However, there is a point at which we can turn the corner, where our focus switches from the past to the future. Our faith helps us turn the corner and then start to look forward.

Faith is about "*being sure of what we hope for and certain of what we do not see*" (Hebrews 11:1). Faith comprises a belief in the fundamental truths of Christianity, together with a trust in the God these describe. Both elements are necessary. Through faith we believe in God, and because of our relationship with Him we can trust in His promises. The sense of purpose and certainty faith brings is based on our trust in God's faithfulness, well founded on the fulfilment of His promises in the Bible and in our own experience. As the psalmist concludes: "*Blessed is the man who makes the Lord his trust*" (Psalm 40:4).

God can be trusted

Faith enables us to go forward when everything around us looks impossible. This is because faith enables us to face the facts of an apparent disaster and look beyond them trusting that, "*in all things God works for the good of those who love him, who have been called according to his purpose*" (Romans 8:28). This is a powerful counter to the shock and sense of failure that redundancy can bring. It places this single event within the larger framework of God's concern over the whole of our lives, past, present and future. We can start to face the facts and our feelings with the reassurance that God's larger plan is in action.

> "By faith Abraham, when called to go to a place he would later receive as his inheritance, obeyed and went, even though he did not know where he was going." Hebrews 11:8

Faith helps us to take things on trust. Abraham did not know his final destination when called by God to leave his country, but was willing to go. Was this a "leap of faith", without knowledge or reasoning? By no means – Abraham knew God and that He could be trusted when all else looked unclear. We can learn from children, whose knowledge of many things is limited; but because they know and trust their mother who has taken care of them in the past, they heed when she says "Don't touch" or "Go this way".

Faith helps us move from deliberation to action. It inspires us with new confidence which comes from learning to rest in God's promises. It helps us to step out and be bold once we perceive God's purpose, despite difficult circumstances or lack of knowledge. Hebrews 11 gives a catalogue of people of faith who, because they trusted God, were moved to action to fulfil His purposes.

For reflection and action

- *Your faith is founded on a God who can be trusted.*
- *As you trust God, you will be able to face facts, take things on trust and take action as you perceive God's purposes working out.*
- *Read Hebrews 11:1–12. What motivated the people mentioned in these verses? Are there things you need to take on trust? Is there a direction God is inviting you to take? Pray for the faith to step out where He is leading.*

The Promise of a Future

Being made redundant can make us feel we no longer have a future, as if someone has cancelled it like the cancelling of some event we were looking forward to. To take away someone's future is to take away their hope, their reason to go on.

Rekindling hope

Hope is essential to human life. Hope is an expectation about a better future. It enables us to continue and not give way to defeat or despair at every hurdle. It is a kind of faith for the future that helps us to endure hardship in the present. Redundancy appears to take away that future, hence smashes hope. How can we rekindle the hope necessary to live again?

We all need hope, but what we hope for will vary greatly from person to person. If our overriding hope is for a comfortable lifestyle, then our hope will certainly be shaken by redundancy since it depends on our earning power. Whilst hoping for such things is part of life, for the Christian they pale into insignificance compared with the hope of eternal life (Colossians 1:27), a hope which is founded on God (1 Timothy 4:9–10).

Hope – an anchor for the soul

Christian hope stretches beyond this life into eternity and so cannot be taken away from us. It creates a total hope within by which all the other hopes of life can align and find their meaning. As the hymn expresses it: "All my hope on God is founded". Christian hope is not the tentative "I hope so" of common usage, but a confident trust in and expectation about the future based on the promises of God.

Where there is despair, God brings hope, the promise of a future. Jeremiah gave God's message to the despondent Jews in exile. He promised to give them *hope and a future* (Jeremiah 29:11). Such promises are found throughout the Bible. We are encouraged to put our hope in His unfailing love (Psalm 147:11). God's record of answering His people with saving deeds makes Him *the hope of all the ends of the earth and of the farthest seas*" (Psalm 65:5).

God is our hope, even when we are made redundant. He has a future for us, which although different from our expectations, will be good for us. We can be confident of this because God is trustworthy; no one who puts their hope in Him will ever be put to shame (Psalm 25:3). Hebrews describes this hope as an anchor for the soul, firm and secure (Hebrews 6:19). It can hold us steady when facing problems, and give us a secure place from which to look ahead. It is the key to us renewing our strength to go on.

For reflection and action

- You have an unshakeable hope founded in God that gives you the promise of a future.
- Drawing on this hope can sustain you in the present and help you to move towards the future.
- Read Isaiah 40:25–31. Draw new strength from the hope that God gives. Ask Him to reassure you of your future and to guide you towards it.

Open to Whatever is Next

When we seek God's plan for our next job, a certain openness is required on our part. Then we can consider all of the possibilities that may exist, and be receptive to the guidance we receive.

To start with, we will probably look for work which will use our skills and experience. Our search can then be broadened, as we all have skills which could be transferred to other types of work, or built upon with extra training. So we need to be open to a wider range of possibilities than perhaps our previous work experience has conditioned us to be. Such openness will help us be more flexible in a world where jobs are changing faster than ever and increased vocational mobility is required of all of us.

A new role

Moses was not keen to take on his new role as leader and spokesman of God's people. He questioned *"Who am I, that I should go to Pharaoh and bring the Israelites out of Egypt?"* (Exodus 3:11). Yet this is what he did, with God's help and a little vocal support from his brother Aaron! His background and experience, skills and abilities were transferred to performing this new role and used by God to great effect.

Openness is required if we are to find God's path for us. If we restrict our thinking to certain narrow areas and remain closed to the rest, we may be in danger of missing God's path. Like on a country walk, if we do not keep our eyes open for the next footpath or the next signpost, we may take the wrong path or get lost and end up spending a lot of time retracing our steps.

The need to be open

As we have seen in the text for today, Isaiah told the Jewish exiles who were in danger of not comprehending where God was leading, to be aware

> **"Forget the former things; do not dwell on the past. See, I am doing a new thing! Now it springs up; do you not perceive it? I am making a way in the desert and streams in the wasteland." Isaiah 43:18–19**

of the new thing God was doing. We, too, need to be open and receptive in this way, and not be hindered by dwelling too much on the past. Our openness demonstrates our trust in God and gives us an enlarged view of the opportunities available. If a particular opportunity fails it is not the end of our world – we are prepared to give God the benefit of the doubt. It is an openness that responds to the call of God to serve Him and others with the response of Isaiah: *"Here am I. Send me!"* (Isaiah 6:8), and hence prepares us for obedience to God's command. It helps us be flexible in a world where jobs are changing fast.

For reflection and action

- You need to be open to new opportunities as doors close on old ones.
- Being receptive to God's leading will help you find His path for your life.
- Read Exodus 3:1–14. Consider Moses' change of direction. Is God leading you in new ways through the experience of redundancy?

Seeking the Way Ahead

Jesus emphasises how we are to pray – with firm faith, asking God for what we need. We are also to seek, i.e. to do everything in our power to receive what we ask for in prayer, and to knock, i.e. to do it urgently and with energy. Applying these principles to looking for another job, we are to ask God to meet our need, to play our part by actively seeking a job and to do both with energy. God's promise is that our need will be met, and the door will be opened.

Seek God first

So we are to actively seek what God would have us do next. However, if our job seeking is to remain in proper perspective, our primary aim must be to seek God Himself first. This places all our seeking within the context of God's will and kingdom. Otherwise we will chase after things to no avail, and only become more anxious. Jesus teaches us not to worry over life's necessities, rather to get our priorities right, and God will see our needs are met: "*But seek first his kingdom and his righteousness, and all these things will be given to you as well*" (Matthew 6:33).

Re-evaluate and investigate

The time between jobs is not wasted time. It is a time of seeking and "pushing doors", a time to re-evaluate skills and investigate new ways to both earn a living and serve God. We will not always get it right en route and may follow some false trails during this time. However, we can trust God to guide us and be reassured that He will have the last word. This does not negate our choice and the responsibility we have for our decisions, but does underline the overall sovereignty of God.

> **"Ask and it will be given to you; seek and you will find; knock and the door will be opened to you."** Luke 11:9

This time is one for exploring and testing the job market: finding out where there are opportunities, writing to companies, applying for jobs, finding out what interest there is in our skills, and where we need to add or develop skills. It is a time for presenting ourselves and our skills to others in ways that do justice to what we have to offer.

For reflection and action

- As you ask for God's help in prayer, you are also to seek the answer. Then, as God promises, you will receive and find.

- The time between jobs is a time for seeking and "pushing the doors" until you find the one that opens for you.

- Read Luke 11:1–13. Read this passage then use its principles to pray about your job search, asking God to meet your need for employment. Put into practice the seeking part through some planned actions including: writing to organisations who may be interested (and in whom you are interested) attaching your CV; finding out which newspapers, journals, etc. advertise the jobs most appropriate, and making sure you have regular access to them; applying to job advertisements – a wide selection at first, then narrowing down as you get an idea of where and at what level your skills are of interest.

Choosing and God's Will

In our job search we will be faced with decisions and choices to be made, and will want to make them in the light of God's will for us. The fact that God has an overall purpose for our lives does not mean we can abdicate responsibility for decisions and accept any situation as the will of God. Each of us has responsibility for our lives and needs to make decisions concerning our future. However, God is sovereign and fulfils His purposes through us.

God's choice – our choice

As we make choices about how to use our skills, God speaks to us to guide us in His purposes for our lives. As we walk closely with Him, our choosing and His will coalesce – this is as it should be as we walk by the Spirit. Then we make choices He would make because we are basing our lives on His priorities and character, and listening to His voice. In so doing, we fulfil God's purposes, as well as doing what is ultimately best for us (Romans 8:28).

God's overall plan

God has an overall sovereign will for the world with purposes that cannot be thwarted (Psalm 96:10). In the fulfilment of these purposes, our work has the potential to be of great service to God and to others. Therefore, our choice of the next job is a very significant decision. It is not like choosing the route we will travel to the shops, which is generally of little consequence, but is something in which God's guidance is usually very specific. Hence, "any old job" will not do – we need to find the role God has for us and make this our choice.

> **"Many are the plans in a man's heart, but it is the Lord's purpose that prevails." Proverbs 19:21**

We have the privilege and the responsibility of choosing. However, our choosing does not put us outside the sphere of God's will and sovereignty. In fact, even though God allows us our choice, He retains ultimate control. Through foolishness or miscalculation, poor judgement or unwise counsel, we make the wrong choice, fall into sin, or take the less than best path, but we cannot step out of the reach of God's overall plan. God's overall purposes will be achieved as God is sovereign and can influence and control events so that His desired ends are achieved.

Coupled to this, God knows us through and through and understands how we are best utilised and fulfilled (Psalm 139:1–3). Hence, when our choosing is coupled with His will, we will find true satisfaction in our work.

For reflection and action

- God is in overall control and you need to trust Him to reveal His purposes.
- It is through walking closely with God that your choosing will align with His purpose.
- Read Romans 8:28–39. What does this passage teach of God at work in our lives and of His love for us? Ask Him to guide you in your choosing, aligning your desires and decisions with His will.

Is the World My Oyster?

We need to approach and investigate opportunities with openness, probing likely options as we seek God's way ahead. We have all heard the saying, "The world is your oyster", as if we have an á la carte menu to choose from. To be realistic, there are various limitations facing each of us. If we view these positively, we can harness them to provide a framework for our search, so that we focus on what is truly possible and best for us. Sometimes we need to reassess such limits, as we may have previously underestimated our abilities.

What are our limits?

One limit is our place in history. We are born in a particular time and place. We have parents we cannot choose and an education, at least initially, that we have little control over. The place and circumstances in which we grow up and live have an influence on the opportunities available and the types of work we seek. These limits are not insurmountable; many a "local boy has made good", and God has a track record of doing mighty things through the lowly. However, they help us understand the situations we find ourselves in, and can prevent us from envy or self-punishment for not matching the achievements of others.

We are also limited by the skills, abilities and inclinations we possess, or are able to develop. There is great flexibility here as we are more capable than we think to learn, or discover and nurture new gifts. Thinking about our limits may help us consider new areas and expand our view of what we are able to do.

> "For you created my inmost being; you knit me together in my mother's womb. I praise you because I am fearfully and wonderfully made; your works are wonderful, I know that full well." Psalm 139:13–14

Realistic dreams

However, there are some things we will probably never be able to do, and others that would merely frustrate us to attempt. If we have no head for figures, accountancy is not for us; if no skill with a ball, then professional football is ruled out; if no ability to impart knowledge, then teaching is not viable, and so on. We can and should dream, but better our dreams are within realistic limits, not totally outside of them. Otherwise we will be continually frustrated and unfulfilled.

For reflection and action

- Your history, skills, gifts and abilities define some limits within which to undertake your job search.
- Remember, such limits are a framework – they help define where your search should focus, but do not determine where it will end.
- Read Psalm 139:1–16. Give thanks to God for the way He has made you, your skills and gifts, your background and history. Ask Him to show you where your limits are so that you will not be frustrated in following unrealistic options, but also to show you where you have unrealised potential that needs tapping.

Questions to Consider

Having a clear idea of our skills, abilities and experience, and the limits upon these, helps us focus our search for the next job. How else can we direct our search in the right direction, or if faced with a number of opportunities, narrow these down? Taking time to consider a number of questions in relation to a job opportunity can help.

Would this job serve God?

Can this job be done for God as part of our service, even worship? This does not restrict us to Christian ministry or the caring professions, as important as these are, since it is possible to serve God in a great variety of jobs. However, it does rule out some areas that are clearly contrary to God's purposes (e.g. burglary!). It also challenges us to probe all opportunities until we are satisfied that they will not involve us in products or methods that are unethical and dishonouring to God. Such a question helps direct us towards jobs that render goods and services that are truly needed or that enrich life, over those that produce trivia that no one really needs, or that generate products that are unnecessarily wasteful or even harmful.

In our searching we need to bear in mind the gifts God has given us and the skills we possess or can develop. The parable of the talents (Matthew 25:14–30) teaches that we are to use the gifts entrusted to us. In fact we will be held accountable for them; the more we have been given, the more will be expected of us. We also need to be open to God leading us in new ways – He knows us better than we know ourselves and may develop unexpected gifts and abilities in us. The Bible gives some powerful examples of people whose aptitudes were expanded through God's command (e.g. Moses, Exodus 3:11–12).

> **"Each one should use whatever gift he has received to serve others, faithfully administering God's grace in its various forms."**
> **1 Peter 4:10**

Am I the person for the job?

Many types of work can be used to serve God, but in a world where many jobs have to remain undone, does God want this particular job done? The related question follows – just because a certain job needs doing, does that mean I am the person to do it? There may be someone better skilled or better suited. Or God may have use for my skills elsewhere.

Money can easily become the major factor in choosing a job. The materialistic pressures of our society are great and can lure us into basing our decisions on the salary offered. This stated, we have a responsibility to our dependants, and others whom God may require us to help. It is right that our work should generate reward for our efforts and skill (Luke 10:7), and enable us to meet the material needs of ourselves and our dependants.

For reflection and action

- *Will this opportunity honour God and use your skills to serve others in some way?*
- *Will it utilise what you do best, support your dependants; and most important, is it what God wants you to do?*
- *Read Matthew 25:14–30. Consider the things you do best. How can they be utilised in your future work to serve God and others?*

Tools to Help (1)

The first tool to help us in our guidance is the Bible. It helps us differentiate right from wrong and sharpens our judgement in deciding between various "good" paths. It is a lamp to our feet and a light to our path (Psalm 119:105). In studying it, we need to use our understanding to weigh up options against biblical principles, and also allow the Spirit to speak to us through it. As the sword of the Spirit (Ephesians 6:17), it has power to penetrate thoughts and actions and help us resolve difficult choices (Hebrews 4:12). As we immerse ourselves in the Bible's principles under the Spirit's leading, we build a godly character, which in many instances will then help us respond to new situations with the "mind of Christ".

God's Word – not a horoscope

While the Bible is an essential tool in our guidance, we must be careful not to misuse it. Picking verses out of context as guidance (or justification) for certain choices can be misleading. We must understand what the passage means in its context, and how to apply its principles elsewhere. Opening the Bible expecting to be led to a particularly significant verse for the decision we have to make is equally dubious. We cannot rule out God guiding us through finding a verse which is particularly relevant to our situation, but to build a model of decision making on a "horoscope" approach is not correct use of God's Word.

Prayer

We are encouraged to bring our concerns, fears and requests before God in prayer (Philippians 4:6; Psalm 55:1–3, 16–17). Through prayer we align our will with God's, clarify the issues on our heart, and in our listening give God the opportunity to speak to us. While we need to be careful of the subjectivity of our own feelings, many can give testimony to incidents where they have experienced an "inner witness", or a "sense of rightness"

"Whether you turn to the right or to the left, your ears will
hear a voice behind you, saying, 'This is the way; walk in it.'"
Isaiah 30:21

about a particular course of action chosen through listening prayer.
This needs testing against biblical principles and other tools (e.g. advice,
circumstances), since it is not difficult to feel led to do something that is
really convenient or we really want to do! Listening prayer can also be a
powerful tool in the context of a worshipping group of Christians where
others can help us listen, test and receive what God is saying.

Where possible, we should bring all the tools God has given to our
decision making, looking for alignment of the results of these tools like
the alignment of runway lights as an aircraft makes its approach.

For reflection and action

- Let your thinking be moulded by biblical principles so
  that you bring these to bear on decisions about jobs.
- Bring everything before God in prayer, listening and
  responding to His leading.
- Read Psalm 119:97–112. Apply biblical principles and
  listening prayer to all the options you are considering.

Tools to Help (2)

Sometimes a new opportunity so obviously fits our skills and abilities that perhaps we should consider whether there are reasons to reject it rather than deliberating whether to accept. However, we need to take care with circumstances as we can easily be driven along by events, or take a particular job just because it appears convenient at the time. David did not look at circumstances alone when Saul's life was effectively delivered into his hands (1 Samuel 24). Rather, he tested the event against other criteria – in this case, God's principles; it was wrong to harm the Lord's anointed.

Guidance

A further way of testing circumstances is to "push the door", e.g. applying for a job, or attending an interview. If the door closes, this can be a useful way of ruling out an option, at least at that time or through that route. If the door opens, this is not necessarily positive guidance, but it does enable us to evaluate the situation with additional information. Circumstances are one factor among others that we must take into account in our choosing, testing them against other guidance, rather than seeing them as conclusive on their own.

We should not be satisfied with our own opinion on difficult decisions, but humble enough to seek counsel and advice (Proverbs 12:15). Seeking out those with greater experience, knowledge or expertise in the area concerned can be very helpful. Speaking with someone who knows us well, who can test our resolve and help us compare our skills and abilities with those required, will help us make a good decision. However, we must remember that no one can choose for us; we have to live with our decisions and are held accountable for them, not our advisors.

Gideon, unsure that he had truly been spoken to by God, laid a fleece on the ground asking for it to be wet and the ground dry the following morning (Judges 6:36–37). Asking God for a "sign" in this way is another way of seeking guidance, although is inappropriate if used as a way of avoiding decisions. In the case of Gideon's fleece, it probably demonstrates a lack of faith on his part – he had already received guidance and wanted to check it (twice!).

Test all guidance

As a rule, Scripture does not encourage us to seek signs to guide us. Where such "direct guidance" is given in the New Testament, it is usually to enlarge understanding of Scripture (e.g. Peter and Cornelius, Acts 10), or to instruct in a way contrary to what appears obvious (Paul called to Macedonia, Acts 16:6–10). Signs are the exception rather than the rule, and usually occur unexpectedly. Of course, God can speak to us in some clear or dramatic way, but we must test all guidance against the other tools.

For reflection and action

- *Seek the advice of others, but remember that the decision remains your own.*
- *Weigh up circumstances and signs with biblical principles, prayer and advice, looking for their alignment.*
- *Read Acts 6:1–6. The "seven" were the obvious choice for the job that needed doing. Are there circumstances or other indicators that point you in a certain direction? What of other guidance you have received? Is there someone who can advise you and help test your ideas?*

Wisdom in Deciding

Being open and seeking guidance will lead us to the point where we will have to make a decision about the next job. When we are offered an opportunity, we have to decide whether this is the right one, or should we continue looking? Is a bird in the hand worth two in the bush? If we are fortunate enough to be offered more than one suitable opportunity that matches our guidance, how do we make a decision?

God's wisdom

We need wisdom to know what is the right decision. Wisdom is a part of God's character, and He specifically promises it to those who ask. However, the wisdom spoken of in the Bible is not "earthly" wisdom, but "heavenly" wisdom (James 3:13–18). This wisdom is not based on human under-standing or experience, but is wisdom that judges situations using God's values and insight – applying a heavenly mind to down-to-earth problems. In deciding on the next job, we not only want to know the best opportunity to pursue, but the one which is aligned with God's values and purposes.

Heavenly wisdom will often confirm what common sense suggests. For example, the job that best matches our skills is often the one that fulfils God's purposes for us. However, sometimes heavenly wisdom overrules what seems obvious as it sees further than we can. Humanly speaking, we may favour taking a job in a large secure company, but heavenly wisdom may guide us to accept a role in a smaller, less stable concern, because this is part of God's plan for us.

> **"If any of you lacks wisdom, he should ask God,
> who gives generously to all without finding fault,
> and it will be given to him." James 1:5**

A gift from God

Wisdom is a gift from God. It grows in us as our relationship with God grows (Proverbs 9:10). We need to let His Spirit work in us (being full of the Spirit and full of wisdom go together, Acts 6:3), and to immerse ourselves in His Word so that the values by which we make judgements and decisions are God's.

Wisdom is more than applying a set of values to situations. The wise person perceives the real nature of situations and how God is at work. Discernment is an aspect of wisdom, that of being able to distinguish between various choices, seeing them not only at face value but how they fit into God's purposes. Discernment is used to test whether words and teaching originate from God's Spirit (1 Corinthians 12; 1 John 4:1–6). It is also to be used for choices concerning our work so that we can determine the right path for us.

For reflection and action

- You need the wisdom that comes from God to help make the right decisions about your future.
- The discernment that accompanies wisdom will help you perceive God's will and choose between different options.
- Read James 3:13–17; Proverbs 2:1–15. Ask for God's wisdom in the decisions you have to make, His discernment as you seek to understand His purposes.

For the Waiting

We often have to wait for a promise to be fulfilled. Children have to wait for the promised gifts at Christmas, which they find unbearable at times! There are no short cuts since opening presents early would spoil their enjoyment of the event. Waiting can be uncomfortable at the best of times, but in our "instant", "buy now, pay later" world it feels very frustrating.

Patience

We need patience to wait for promises to be fulfilled. Many of God's promises concern the future, such as Jesus' return: "*Be patient, then, brothers, until the Lord's coming*" (James 5:7). Some of God's promises, however, are fulfilled in this life – God promised to bless Abraham and to give him many descendants: "*And so after waiting patiently, Abraham received what was promised*" (Hebrews 6:15). We are instructed to "*imitate those who through faith and patience inherit what has been promised*" (Hebrews 6:12).

In quietness and confidence

Patience is ranked high among the qualities a Christian is encouraged to develop with God's help. It is described as one of the fruits of the Spirit (Galatians 5:22), as an outworking of love (1 Corinthians 13:4), and is almost always mentioned when Christian virtues are listed (e.g. Ephesians 4:2; Colossians 3:12). Patience is not a fatalistic resignation when faced with insurmountable problems. Rather, it is a quiet and confident waiting which trusts in the perfect timing and providence of God. It is closely linked to hope, which provides the promise of the future for which patience waits (Romans 8:24–25). Without it, hope can slip back into despair.

If our period of unemployment drags on and our attempts to find another job are unsuccessful, we need to learn to "*Be joyful in hope, patient in affliction ...*" (Romans 12:12). Patience helps us to put aside

> **"I waited patiently for the Lord; he turned to me and heard my cry. He lifted me out of the slimy pit, out of the mud and mire; he set my feet on a rock and gave me a firm place to stand." Psalm 40:1**

the disappointments, using them as experience gained while waiting to grasp the right opportunity. It also helps us to find rest and peace instead of the turmoil and panic which can so easily overwhelm. The advice of the psalmist is sound: "*Be still before the Lord and wait patiently for him; do not fret when men succeed in their ways, when they carry out their wicked schemes*" (Psalm 37:7).

The experience of those who practise patience is expressed in Psalm 40:1 – God hears us and gives us a firm place to stand when all else appears to be shifting and unstable.

For reflection and action

- Patience is necessary for the waiting period before God's promise is fulfilled.
- It helps us put aside disappointments and find peace until the right opportunity is found.
- Read Psalm 40:1–8. Think about the relationship between patience, trust and God's will described in these verses. Use it as a prayer, asking God to grant you patience. List some of the things that have happened to you during your job search so far. From these experiences, think through how you are going to approach the time ahead, practising patience.

Keeping Going

Unemployment is like a long distance run, requiring the stamina, endurance and determination of a marathon runner. It is not usually a sprint, where one big effort culminates in another job. It is more like a grinding course where the finishing line is a long way off, and usually out of sight until we get near to it. During unemployment we need to keep going despite the setbacks, the prolonged uncertainty and the challenges to self-esteem and confidence. We need persistence to write another letter, complete another job application and go to another interview if our job search is to continue through to completion.

Perseverance

Patience can keep us peaceful in the waiting period and help us cope with disappointments. Perseverance is needed to keep us going; it is steadfast pursuit of an aim. It combines both endurance (ability to withstand) and courage (willing to bravely face difficulties). As with patience, it is often listed with other Christian qualities (e.g. 2 Peter 1:6; Romans 5:4), and is used in Paul's description of love (love "always perseveres", 1 Corinthians 13:7). As it states in Hebrews; "*You need to persevere so that when you have done the will of God, you will receive what he has promised*" (Hebrews 10:36).

Perseverance is inspired, fuelled and strengthened by hope. They are so inter-related that perseverance in its turn yields increased hope: "*... but we also rejoice in our sufferings, because we know that suffering produces perseverance; perseverance, character; and character, hope*" (Romans 5:3–4). Perseverance helps us survive until the future promise is fulfilled. It also has positive benefits in the present as it develops our character. James states that the testing of our faith through trials builds our perseverance, and that "*Perseverance must finish its work so that you may be mature and complete,* *not lacking anything*" (James 1:4). It is amazing that God can bring us through a trial such as redundancy and make us more mature and complete because of it.

Keep your eyes on Jesus

The writer to the Hebrews pictures us in a race. He encourages us to put off everything that hinders and to keep going (Hebrews 12:1). What is the secret of getting to the finishing line? It is fixing our eyes on Jesus and using Him as our model of perseverance, so that we will not grow weary or lose heart (Hebrews 12:2–3).

For reflection and action

- *With God's help, persevere through the trial of redundancy so that you will see His promises fulfilled.*
- *As you persevere, allow God to work in you, making you more mature and complete in Him.*
- *Read James 1:2–12; Hebrews 12:1–3; 10:35–39. James addresses Christians going through trials and suffering, reassuring them that they will receive the promise as they persevere. How can you make this real in your situation? Use Hebrews 12:1–3 to reflect on Jesus and His endurance. Ask God to develop such perseverance in your life and to bring other fruit through the experience of redundancy.*

Drawing Strength

Redundancy brings pressures we may not have faced before. It attacks us in many ways: spiritually, as our faith undergoes trials; materially, as it threatens our security; and emotionally, as our self-esteem and confidence are undermined. It is a multi-faceted assault, like a castle being attacked from all sides at the same time. It is not usually a single blow, but more like a lengthy siege that has the potential to break down the walls through constant pressure.

God's strength

It is possible to soldier on in our own strength, but we risk being exhausted and overwhelmed. It can make us weak and vulnerable when we need to be strong and decisive. To survive we need to draw on a strength deeper than our own – as Christians, we know that such strength is available in God.

We need God to be our strength. When our enemies are drawn up against us on every side, and the odds are stacked against us, we need God's help. Psalm 3 depicts such a situation. Like the psalmist, as we call on God, He becomes our fortress in which to take refuge, and our shield around us. God acts on our behalf, demonstrating His strength and power through working in the situation and delivering us.

Our God is all-powerful

As well as acting on our behalf, God imparts some of His great strength to us. The everlasting God, the Creator of the universe, is all powerful, and He gives His strength and power to us when we are under attack or weary (Isaiah 40:28–31). The apostle Paul faced pressures from all sides (see

2 Corinthians 6:4–10 and 11:22–29 for the extent of the pressures on him).
How did he cope? He drew on a deeper strength, strength within given by
God, enabling him to face any situation.

For reflection and action

- God is a shield around you in times of trouble. He is your strength, acting on your behalf.
- He imparts His strength to you, so that in His strength you can face pressures from all sides and not be overwhelmed by them.
- Read Psalm 18:1–15, 32–36. Ask God to be your fortress at this time, to act on your behalf, and like a shield to protect you from attacks on all sides (vv.1–6). Use verses 7–15 to remind yourself of God's power. Read verses 16–19 and envision how His power will bring about your rescue. In what areas of your life do you need God to specifically arm you with His strength (vv.32–36)?

By the Spirit

We will handle the crisis of redundancy best if we draw on the strength that God provides through the Holy Spirit. The Spirit grants His power to meet particular needs, anointing and filling people to overflowing. There are many Old Testament examples of the Spirit's power being given to perform particular deeds (e.g. Gideon, Judges 6:34) or to fulfil a particular role (e.g. David, 1 Samuel 16:13). The risen Jesus told His disciples that they would receive power when the Holy Spirit came upon them (Acts 1:8). This power transformed them from dismayed individuals into a witnessing church. The Spirit's power equips people for life and ministry (1 Corinthians 12:1–11). During redundancy we need an outpouring of the Spirit's power, as if standing beneath a waterfall of God's blessing, experiencing its force and its refreshment.

Be filled with His Spirit

The Spirit also works to make us more like Christ. This is the sanctifying work of the Spirit (2 Thessalonians 2:13), producing fruit in our lives (Galatians 5:22), and transforming us into the likeness of Christ (2 Corinthians 3:18). As Paul prayed for the Ephesians, we need God to strengthen us with power through His Spirit in our inner being (Ephesians 3:16). The Spirit's work in us is like a well within that supplies us with whatever we need to go on.

It is the Spirit who guides us in the truth, teaching us about God and how to do what is right (John 14:26; 16:13). In Paul's words, as we live by the Spirit, we need to keep in step with the Spirit (Galatians 5:25). Keeping in step with the Spirit is important for all our decision-making – as we seek with openness the future path for us, we need to listen to His prompting. Just as the churches in Revelation had to listen to what the Spirit had to say to them if they were to progress, so do we. This may come in many ways, sometimes in dramatic fashion, or sometimes like a gentle whisper (1 Kings 19:12).

He helps us with our prayers

As a child we turned to Mum or Dad when something went wrong. For life's trials, God as our heavenly Father wants us to turn to Him. The Spirit helps us do this, reassuring us of God's parenthood so that we pray "Abba, Father" and bring to Him in childlike trust our worries (Romans 8:15–16). When faced with the facts of redundancy, it is often difficult to know where to start in prayer – so much has been lost, so much affected. The Spirit understands our deepest needs and helps us with our prayers. In fact, He intercedes for us in accordance with God's will so that as we pray we are aligning ourselves with God's purposes, and thus will hear more clearly His voice in guidance (Romans 8:26–27).

For reflection and action

- Ask for the Spirit's power to come upon you and to work within you as you handle the trials caused by redundancy.
- Pray in the Spirit so that you may know God's fatherly care and be attuned to His guidance for your life.
- Read Ephesians 3:14–21. Make this prayer your own. Ask God to help you to be more open to His working in your life so that your handling of redundancy will truly be "by the Spirit".

Using Time

We may suddenly have lots of time on our hands through being made redundant. Time, that commodity always in short supply when in work, is now ours in abundance. But it may be unwelcome, as we would rather be doing other things such as earning our keep or continuing our career. This time comes unstructured and in long stretches, rather than in the well-ordered format of work. From the frantic pace of work, where an hour's free time is a bonus, we can find ourselves facing seemingly endless days of empty time. It is easy to feel we are merely marking time, or worse, that our lives are being wasted.

The gift of time

The life given to us by God is one of His greatest gifts to us (Genesis 2:7). It is uniquely ours; no one else can live our lives for us, or use the time we have. Our responsibility is to use time in ways that please and serve God (Colossians 3:23–24). We may protest that through redundancy the opportunity to use our time and gifts profitably has been taken away. Certainly, the way of serving Him in our former job has been removed, but this does not release us from the responsibility and privilege of serving Him in our new situation.

A time for everything

The writer of Ecclesiastes points out that there is a time for everything – every activity and phase of our lives has its season (Ecclesiastes 3:1). We may experience a time of work and a time of unemployment. In whatever circumstances we find ourselves, we are to make the most of our time. We can do this if we trust God with what is happening to us, placing our time into His hands.

The change from the busy routine of work to the unstructured state of unemployment can throw us into such disarray that even getting up in the mornings is a major effort. We need to organise our time by establishing a new structure for the day and the week. Our main purpose will become the search for the next job – a major project in its own right that many liken to a full-time task! There will be other purposes, like developing new skills to equip us better for future roles. There is also the opportunity to do some of the things we have never had the time to do before: jobs around the house; seeing friends. By keeping active and purposeful, our self-confidence will be retained and we can help encourage those around us also affected by our redundancy.

For reflection and action

- Your time is a gift from God to be used in His service in whatever you do.
- Faced with an abundance of empty time, you need to organise it and give it purpose, making good use of it in between jobs.
- Read Ecclesiastes 3:1–8. How can you make the time you are now in "quality" time rather than "empty" time? Make a plan for tomorrow, listing some things you want to achieve. Schedule events over the next couple of weeks, some to progress your job search (which is your new "full-time" work), and some to ensure you remain in touch with friends, have fellowship and get support.

Shoulders to Lean On

Being made redundant is difficult enough, without feeling isolated as well. Redundancy removes us from the working environment where many of our friends are, and places us at home when many of our friends and family are out at work. A plaque on my parents' bedroom wall reads "A life without friends is like a garden without flowers". More than ever in times of crisis, we need to call on the support of friends and family, those close to us whom we love, trust and can rely on.

Let others in

We need to turn to those who will listen as we adjust to changed horizons, face our fears and find the way forward. Good listeners will understand, reassure us of our value, help rebuild our confidence, mourn with us when we are sad and rejoice with us when we are happy (Romans 12:15). They can help us see the positive in our situation and the good that might come of it, so that we can face the present difficulties. When we need to receive love which protects, trusts, hopes and perseveres (1 Corinthians 13:7), God can use them to bring it.

Bouncing ideas off family or friends who know us well can help us see situations more objectively. The people who know us best can speak frankly with us and help see more clearly. Those who care for us and share our faith are concerned that we find God's purposes, and can be used as God's instruments in guiding our choosing.

A tower of strength

Those who are closest to us are those who will love us at all times, in trial or in joy, unemployed or employed, ill or healthy, poor or rich. In the Old Testament, David's friendship with Jonathan was tested when his life was in danger from Jonathan's father, King Saul. The friendship proved to be a tower of strength as their oneness of spirit and love for each other gave mutual support in adverse circumstances (1 Samuel 20).

Jesus called His disciples His friends (John 15:15), and cited the greatest example of love as someone who is willing to lay down their life for their friends (John 15:13). He shared some of the most significant events of His life with His friends. When in deepest distress in the Garden of Gethsemane, He valued the presence of His closest friends as He prayed (Mark 14:32–34).

For reflection and action

- Do not keep your anxieties or your hopes to yourself – express them to someone you know will listen, and who will help you test your plans for the future.
- No one is an island – good friends are towers of strength when the going is tough.
- Read 1 Samuel 18:1–4. Think about your close family and friends, those whom you trust, and with whom you have an understanding. If redundancy has cut you off from some of your close friends, find ways of renewing contact. Resolve not to become isolated through this experience, but rather to deepen and strengthen your friendships.

Finding Fellowship

The demands of work can make us take the church family for granted, and sometimes view it as an additional demand on our time. When redundant we realise how enriching its wider circle of fellowship, contact and support actually is. The church brings God's love to us in many different ways. We should not feel guilty about receiving such support, but accept it in the grace in which it is given, recognising that it is a natural outworking of Christ's love through His people.

Receiving from God's people

We need to be able to share our experiences with those who have been through a similar ordeal and benefit from wise advice. At times we need enthusing with the energy and drive of the young and to learn the simple trust of a child. We may also need the objectivity of someone who knows nothing of our job situation, but who can perceive God's purposes at work. At other times, we need to lay aside our needs in order to help another, to give out as well as to receive. We often need to supplement our gifts and experience with those of others, making up what we lack.

It is unlikely that our close circle of family and friends will meet all of these requirements but the church family consists of a diverse group of people with a vast array of differing gifts, abilities and experience. Paul likens the church to a body with many parts, Christ as its head. All the parts are interdependent (just as the eye needs the hand, and the head needs the feet), hence all are indispensable if the body is to function well (1 Corinthians 12:12–26). The range of gifts and experience represented in our own local church will surprise us, and these are resources lovingly offered in service to God and one another.

Christ's love within the church

It is Christ's love that holds the church together and helps it to grow (Ephesians 4:15–16). In addition to flowing out to the world, this love flows within the church, encouraging a deep caring of one another (Romans 12:9–13; 1 Peter 4:8–11), and a willingness to carry one another's burdens.

The support and counsel offered is not only the wisdom of wide and varied experience, but also the result of hearts committed to and seeking God's purposes. In such a worshipping community, the Spirit can work powerfully, helping us to find God's will for the future.

For reflection and action

- The church contains a wide range of gifts and experience, including your own, that, joined together in love, serve to enact God's purposes on earth.

- Your own church is a source of varied forms of support in times of need.

- Read Romans 12:1–8. Thank God for the different people in your church and the range of gifts they possess. Be ready to receive as well as to play your role in the upbuilding of the church, remembering that God uses all members of His body to channel His love.

Presenting Ourselves

The knock to self-esteem caused by redundancy can make us feel unsure of our abilities and unconfident in presenting ourselves. We can feel that people regard us suspiciously because we have been made redundant, and this adds to our feelings of inadequacy. How can we present ourselves in a way that does justice to the skills, abilities and experience we have to offer?

Accept yourself

God's command is to love your neighbour as yourself (Leviticus 19:18; Matthew 22:39). While the focus of this principle is loving others, the phrase "as yourself" indicates that love of self is good and right. Such love is not a proud, selfish love that overlooks sin. Rather, it is a love that accepts ourselves as God accepts us. We are made in His image, forgiven and cleansed from sin through Christ. If God accepts and loves us, then we have secure grounds to accept and love ourselves, and thereby be at peace with ourselves.

If we are at peace with ourselves, we are no longer afraid to face the facts about ourselves – our limitations and our strengths. As Paul says, we are to think of ourselves no more highly than we ought, but with sober judgement, i.e. openly and honestly. This allows us to be comfortable with our abilities, confident about what we can do, and realistic about what we cannot.

Christians are often reticent to advertise their own strengths for fear of being mistaken as arrogant or proud. Vanity, pride and arrogance are certainly to be avoided. However, in our zeal to be humble, we are in danger of sin of a different kind – that of devaluing ourselves, or even misrepresenting our ability. Humility is not about putting ourselves down, but about raising our evaluation of others (Romans 12:10). Jesus was humble but was not afraid to speak the truth about Himself (e.g. John 8:12), describe His skills and characteristics (e.g. Luke 4:18–21) or declare what He could do for others (Matthew 11:28).

Telling it as it is

In our search for the next job we have to present ourselves confidently and clearly, both on paper (letters, CV) and in person. Otherwise, how will a prospective employer know what we can do? As Christians we will not want to promote our abilities in an untruthful or exaggerated way, but using sober judgement, telling it as it is. This includes being straightforward about our achievements and strengths, as well as being open about the difficulties we have faced and how we have coped with them.

For reflection and action

- Love and value yourself as God loves and values you.
- Do not be afraid of presenting your skills and abilities to others – it can be done in a way that neither devalues you, nor boasts.
- Read Romans 5:1–8. Ask God to help you to be at peace with Him and with yourself, recognising that He loves and accepts you through Christ. Think how best to present your skills and abilities.

Serving

To handle redundancy we need to draw deeply on God's strength and the support of family, friends and church. However, as with most situations in life, we are most fulfilled when we are able to give as well as receive. Our service to God and others does not cease when we lose our jobs, although its nature may change. In fact, some of those close to us may need our support more than ever when we are unemployed, as they too are having to cope with the pressures redundancy causes.

Serving God

Whatever we do, we are to do it to the best of our ability because we are ultimately serving God. Even in redundancy and unemployment, our daily activity is to be rendered as service to God. This can be through all manner of activity, from the way we undertake our job search, to the help offered to others in need (Matthew 25:34–40). We must never lose sight of the fact that in all our activity it is God whom we are serving.

We do need to find a job which will pay us sufficient to live and support our dependants. But it is easy to fall into the trap of seeking the best-paid job. This may cause us to rule out opportunities which we think are poorly paid, or to apply for unsuitable jobs merely because of their attractive salary. We need to be reminded of whom we serve, and that we cannot serve two masters; in Jesus' words, we cannot serve both God and Money (Matthew 6:24).

Serving others

Our example is Christ, who came not to be served, but to serve (Matthew 20:26–28). Facing many pressures and the prospect of an untimely death, He continued to serve, donning a towel and performing the humblest of

> **"Whatever you do, work at it with all your heart, as working for the Lord, not for men, since you know that you will receive an inheritance from the Lord as a reward. It is the Lord Christ you are serving." Colossians 3:23–24**

roles (John 13:1–17). Paul teaches that our attitude should be the same as that of Christ (Philippians 2:4–7). This does not mean that we neglect our own situation, but should also look to the interests of others. As well as providing support for them, this helps prevent us becoming self-centred, or worse, self-pitying and totally absorbed with our own plight. It puts our own situation in perspective and teaches us something of how others handle their difficulties. Those close to us need our support during redundancy. We have the responsibility to serve them in their need. At home this means finding ways to ease rather than increase the burdens on them.

For reflection and action

- In good times and in bad it remains your duty and privilege to serve God in whatever you do.
- Giving and receiving belong together. As you are supported in difficult times, it is right (and beneficial) to reach out and serve others in their need.
- Read John 13:1–17. Think of ways you can serve and support those affected by your redundancy. Pray for wisdom about how to support others in need.

Finding Peace

Finding peace amid the turmoil that redundancy causes may sound like a contradiction in terms. Our world is being wrenched apart around us, and the things we took for granted have been swept away by a relentless torrent of change. The reassuring news is that peace can be found, like the quiet refuge found in the eye of the storm. How do we find this peace and rest in it, whatever problems and difficulties we face?

Our future is secure in God

Hope and trust are two essential ingredients to finding peace (Romans 15:13). Having our hope rekindled helps cultivate peace as we grasp the fact that there is a future for us. We sleep better at night knowing the future is secure in God's hands. Trust in God helps us cope with the problems, fears and pressures – we do not run away from them, but can entrust them into God's capable hands and find peace.

Let the peace of Christ rule ...

We need to turn to God as the source of our hope, the One in whom we can trust. Jesus invites us to come to Him and find rest for our souls (Matthew 11:28–30). He grants us His peace, through His Spirit (the Comforter), to keep us from anxiety and fear (John 14:25–27). Peace is a characteristic of the Spirit at work establishing God's kingdom (Romans 14:17), and as part of His kingdom, we are to let the peace of Christ rule in our hearts (Colossians 3:15).

God's peace is not simply physical rest, nor just getting our mind off things for a while through another distraction. It is a deeper peace than these, a peace that, recognising problems are still present, gives us rest amid them. It is the peace that enabled Jesus to rest in the boat while the storm

> "Come to me, all you who are weary and burdened, and I will give you rest. Take my yoke upon you and learn from me, for I am gentle and humble in heart, and you will find rest for your souls. For my yoke is easy and my burden is light." Matthew 11:28–30

raged about Him (Matthew 8:23–27). Based on a supreme confidence in God, it is truly a peace that passes understanding, and that has the power to protect our hearts and minds (Philippians 4:7).

To make this peace ours we come to God open to receive. We come through prayer, bringing our anxieties to Him, and His promise is that we will receive and experience His peace. And, perhaps a little surprisingly at first, we will also be touched by His joy again, as this is what peace brings with it. Thus, even at the beginning of the tunnel of redundancy there is light.

For reflection and action

- Amid the storm you can find peace, a resting place in God.
- God's peace will guard your heart and mind, giving rest, and bringing joy.
- Read Philippians 4:4–9. Taking the advice of these verses, lay out everything about your redundancy before God – the anxieties and hurts, as well as the hopes and opportunities. Give Him thanks and make your requests known, your needs and the desires of your heart. Then rest in His peace and know His joy.

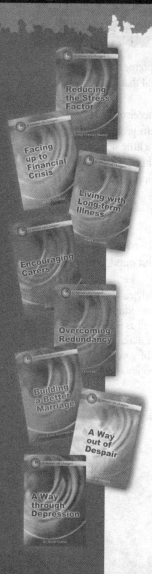

Each title presented in a pack of 6 at £5.94

(equivalent to 99p each)

Previously published as the New Perspectives series.

Reducing the Stress Factor
Learn how to deal with stress biblically and effectively.
ISBN: 1-85345-217-3

Facing up to Financial Crisis
Learn how to deal with finances from a biblical perspective.
ISBN: 1-85345-214-9

Living with a Long-term Illness
Discover how to also live in the truth that "...in all things God works for the good of those who love Him."
ISBN: 1-85345-222-X

Overcoming Redundancy
Face this difficult time by taking the initiative and celebrating your God-given gifts. ISBN: 1-85345-216-5

A Way out of Despair
Address issues of despair, including suicide, rejection, guilt, self-hate. ISBN: 1-85345-218-1

Encouraging Carers
This book helps carers to understand that their strength can b found in God. ISBN: 1-85345-219-X

Building a Better Marriage
A helpful aid for people experiencing a difficult patch, or more serious issues in their marriage. ISBN: 1-85345-213-0

A Way through Depression
Biblical wisdom to help anyone suffering from this debilitating condition. ISBN: 1-85345-221-1